OSBERN'S LIFE OF ALFEGE

For
the Parish Church of St Alfege, Greenwich

FRANCES SHAW

Osbern's
Life of Alfege

ST PAULS

ST PAULS Publishing
Morpeth Terrace, London SW1P 1EP, UK

Copyright (English Translation) © ST PAULS 1999

ISBN 085439 574 1

Set by TuKan, High Wycombe
Produced in the EC
Printed by Biddles Ltd., Guildford, Surrey

ST PAULS is an activity of the priests and brothers
of the Society of St Paul who proclaim the Gospel
through the media of social communication

Acknowledgements

I would like to thank a number of people for their help and encouragement. Particular thanks are due to Dr Alan Thacker of the Institute of Historical Research for allowing me access to unpublished work of his and for time spent in discussion; also to Fr Alfege, Prinknash Abbey and Prof Robert Parker, as well as staff at the British Library and Lambeth Palace Library, for their help in locating material. I am grateful to the Rt Revd Dr George Carey, Archbishop of Canterbury, for permission to quote from his enthronement sermon. Finally, I should like to thank the Revd Canon Giles Harcourt, Vicar of St Alfege, Greenwich, for his support of this project.

Contents

Introduction

In September 1011, some time between the 8th and 29th, Danish raiders who had already overrun much of southern England, attacked the city of Canterbury. They succeeded in their siege through the treachery of a man called Aelfmar, whose life had been saved by Alfege, Archbishop of Canterbury. Alfege himself was taken prisoner, an event recorded in one of the very few pieces of verse in the Anglo-Saxon Chronicle:

Captive then was
He that once
Was head of all England,
Of Christendom.
There could be seen
Great misery
Where formerly
Great joy was seen,
In the city from which
Christianity came,
And bliss before God
And bliss before the world.

On Easter Day of the following year he was brutally murdered at the Danish camp at

Greenwich, so becoming – as Thomas Becket referred to him in his last sermon – 'Canterbury's first Martyr'.

The sources for his life however are sparse. While the Anglo-Saxon Chronicle gives a full account of the events of 1011 and 1012 which culminated in Alfege's death, prior to that it records only brief details such as his translation to the see of Winchester and of Canterbury. Thietmar, Bishop of Merseberg in the 11th century, gives an account of his life and death which he claims to have had from a man who had just come from England. However although his account of his death largely bears out Osbern's version, he curiously confuses Alfege with St Dunstan in parts of his account and has little to say of his early life. Some details of his time at Winchester can be gleaned from Wulfstan's *Narratio*; however it is to Osbern[1], a monk of Christ Church Canterbury, that one must turn for a full and colourful account of the saint's life.

Osbern's account was written in 1070 at the instigation of Archbishop Lanfranc. As we shall see, he had a particular agenda for the work, which to some extent affects its contents and which some may feel undermines its veracity.

When Lanfranc arrived in 1070 at Canterbury from the abbey at Bec, he was dismayed at much of what he found there, in particular the cult of local saints canonised by local acclamation, whose sanctity was supported by little or no documentation. Fire had damaged the cathedral in 1067 and Lanfranc set about restoring the fabric of the building; at the same time he sought to reform the liturgy and restore what he felt was a proper emphasis in the worship. The old cathedral had been built in the style of St Peter's at Rome, and like its model was organised internally in relation to the saints whose relics were held there. St Wilfrid was in the altar at the easternmost end, with an Irish hermit St Fursey in the crypt below him; Oda and Alfege were either side of the altar, Dunstan in a position between the high altar and the choir and a virgin saint Austroberta in the western apse. St Swithun's head also was in the altar: Alfege had brought this from Winchester on his enthronement in 1006. The model for the new cathedral was St Stephen's, Caen, and new locations for the relics resulted from the re-ordering. As Gibson[3] comments, the layout of Lanfranc's cathedral concentrated the attention on universal Christian doctrines rather than local saints. No disrespect was done to the relics – Osbern[4] records that they were removed and re-interred with all due ceremony during the rebuilding. However Lanfranc wanted to regularise their position: the reliquaries were opened and the contents listed[5] to verify their authenticity; at the same time he sought to remedy the lack of documentation by commissioning accounts of their lives.

Even prior to Lanfranc, Canterbury Cathedral was no stranger to changes in liturgy, as is evidenced by the Bosworth and Arundel Psalters with their attached calendars of feast days. The Bosworth Calendar (dated some time between 988 and 1008) is largely that of Glastonbury together with the addition of feast days of some local Kentish saints. It may be supposed therefore that this reflects the observations instituted by Dunstan, who

11

came from Glastonbury to Canterbury. The Arundel Psalter can be dated to between 1012 and 1023 since it marks the death of Alfege, which took place in 1012, but not the feast of his translation – his relics were taken to Canterbury in 1023 – though this feast is recorded in a 12th century addition to the Calendar. When compared with the Bosworth Psalter, it is clear that an extensive reform of the liturgy took place at some between these dates. The later calendar is more akin to that of Winchester than Glastonbury, so may have originated with Alfege himself. However a more significant change is the dropping from the calendar of the saints who comprised the early archbishops buried in the neighbouring priory of St Augustine. Of all the saints invoked in the prayers at the end of the manuscript, Dunstan and Alfege are the only two local saints. The Harleian Canterbury Benedictional too gives particular emphasis to Dunstan and Alfege, allotting them five benedictions each. From this it is argued[6] that Christ Church in its rivalry with the neighbouring community of St Augustine's was attempting to promote its own saints over and against theirs. Osbern's fulsome references to Christ Church may be spiced by this rivalry as much as by fondness for his own community. Lanfranc's suspension of the cults of Dunstan and Alfege should be seen therefore not as the personal distaste of a Norman for Saxon saints, but a bureaucratic concern for regularising their position: to someone used to the legalistic customs at Bec and Cluny local acclamation was insufficient grounds for canonisation. Nevertheless, given the prominence accorded both these saints in the Arundel Psalter, it is easy to guess how the actions of this 'new broom'[7] must have rankled.

An interesting account of Lanfranc's conversation with Anselm in relation to this is told in Eadmer's 'Life of Anselm'.[8] Lanfranc asked Anselm whether Alfege could properly be counted as a martyr given the circumstances of his death: he had, after all, been killed not for professing the faith but because he refused to pay ransom money to his pagan captors. Anselm's reply is a model of sophistry: 'It is clear that a man who has no hesitation in dying rather than sin against God even in a small matter, would very much rather die than anger God by committing some grave sin.' Alfege, he argues, died for the sake of justice: he continues 'He who dies for justice dies for Christ'[9] – hence he is a martyr, since the Church defines a martyr precisely as one who dies for Christ.

Eadmer records that Lanfranc was thoroughly persuaded by this argument: 'I trust that I shall, by God's good grace, henceforth worship and venerate Saint Alfege with all my heart, as a truly great and glorious martyr of Christ.' However, both Eadmer and Osbern add their own arguments to support Alfege's claim to martyrdom, giving as an additional reason for his capture and death that he attempted to convert the Danes when they were burning Canterbury. It was then that Lanfranc ordered the history of his life and passion to be written. Eadmer adds that Osbern wrote it 'not only in plain prose for reading but also put it to music for singing'; in fact, it is clear from Osbern's preface that the hymn was written first. This hymn, outlining the events of the saint's life and passion, would have been sung at one or more of the festivals of St Alfege. It is unfortunately lost, but one can form an impression of what it may have been like from Eadmer's long hymn for St Dunstan's day[10] which is probably of a similar type. Osbern was noted for his musical ability, and his liking for richness of language and ear for musical rhythm is evident even from his prose account.

The circumstances in which Osbern came to write his work may account for a number of features in it, such as the insistence on Alfege's status as a martyr, the portrayal of Alfege as a strict enforcer of discipline, the linkage Osbern makes between Alfege and Dunstan and the interdependence of their sanctity, and finally the comparison between Alfege and established martyrs SS Lawrence and Stephen. In an examination of the relationship between England and the continent in the making of saint-bishops, David Rollason[11] identifies three characteristic aspects of hagiography: the aim (to establish the claim to sanctity), the use of a schema and accounts of miracles and visions in support of the claim. The Popes in the 10th century were demanding accounts of lives and miracles to attest sanctity: Lanfranc's demands on Osbern can be seen as in line with this trend. Rollason cites Zoepf's schema in his analysis of 10th century German saints' lives. Typical elements include the saint's universal popularity from his earliest years, his love of learning, testing by Satan, restoration of churches and monasteries; he cares for the poor, brings peace, visits Rome; finally he dies a holy death which is followed by miracles at the grave. It can be seen that Osbern's *Life of Alfege* conforms fairly closely to this schema.

Although we are told very little about his early life, Alfege is shown to have remarkable gifts from the outset in his aptitude for learning and his devotion to God. His asceticism is a key theme: after his initial few years in the monastic life, he found the priory at Deerhurst too comfortable and sought a more austere regime at Bath. Even here he withdrew to a private cell where he could live still more rigorously, much as St Cuthbert did at Lindisfarne. At Winchester he would stand all night in prayer, ignoring cold and weariness, and fasted to such an extent that daylight could be seen through his clasped hands, (provided, Osbern adds with a note of bathos, that he was standing in front of a window on a bright day.)

Alfege's austerity is contrasted explicitly with the behaviour of the some of the monks at Bath whose lapse into greed and lust is punished by the death of one of their number: on the day after his burial, Alfege witnesses his torment by demons at the scene of his crimes. Osbern may have an additional purpose[12] in relating this rather bizarre story. It clearly portrays Alfege as a reforming influence in the community – a detail which would find favour with Lanfranc, and may be seen too in the context of hostility between lay clerks and monks of the late 10th century at Christ Church Canterbury.

Osbern is at pains to show that each stage of Alfege's career is a step along the path to his eventual destiny of martyrdom. He was appointed to the Bishopric of Winchester after Andrew the

Apostle visited Dunstan, who was at that time Archbishop of Canterbury. Similarly Alfege succeeded to the Archbishop's throne at Canterbury as a direct result of St Dunstan's prayers. However, he was not Dunstan's immediate successor, and Osbern addresses this point arguing that it shows divine providence at work. The appointment of Alfege to Archbishop of Canterbury took place at the time it did, he argues, in order (i) to show how much God loved Dunstan, in that he was fulfilling a promise made to him long after his death, but more particularly (ii) to ensure that Alfege would be at Canterbury when the Danes invaded and so would meet his fate. Again, when Osbern relates the events of Alfege's capture and imprisonment, he places them in the context of Satan's scheming to deprive Alfege of his rightful crown of martyrdom. Edric's conspiracy with the Danes to overthrow Ethelred is prompted by Satan in his malice against Alfege. It is for this reason too that Satan tries to lure Alfege away from prison and martyrdom.

Osbern also invites comparison of Alfege with undoubted martyrs in support of his claim to martyrdom. When the Danes demand a ransom of sixty talents of silver for his release and insist that he signs a document to raise the money from the church's goods Alfege refuses, citing St Lawrence's hiding of church treasures from plunderers as his precedent. Following the account of his death, Osbern equates Alfege with St Stephen, the first martyr. 'Whose merits were ever so comparable as those of this our champion and Stephen the first martyr? For both refused to plunder Church funds, both were most forceful in curtailing evil deeds.' This parallel with St Stephen may account for a curious discrepancy in Osbern's account of the murder compared with that given elsewhere. The Anglo-Saxon Chronicle records that the archbishop was brought before the Danes who had been feasting and were already drunk. Angry at his refusal to have any ransom paid, they fell upon him with 'bones and horns of oxen', presumably from their feast, until one man (named as 'Thrum' in Florence's account) took his axe and killed him. Osbern however makes no mention of ox-bones: in his account the Danes set about him with axe-hafts and stones. Osbern must have known this distinctive detail and it is unlikely that he altered his account on grounds of taste, as lurid details abound elsewhere (– the fiends' torment of the dead sinning monk at Bath, for example). However his version makes Alfege's death far more similar to that of St Stephen and justifies his referring to them both as 'comparable in the manner of their death, equal in the love of their friends... both stones of the sanctuary, trampled by the feet of passers-by, now joined with Christ, the highest cornerstone.'

Miracles as well as visions attest to Alfege's sanctity. When he was attacked and robbed on his way to Rome, fire miraculously threatened the town of his assailants; equally miraculously Alfege succeeded in diverting the fire away from the town out of compassion for the people. Before leaving Rome, Alfege had an accurate premonition of Kenwuld's death. Osbern declines to describe the miracles he performed while archbishop of Canterbury, but his account ends with the

17

remarkable miracle of the oarblade, which sprouted when dipped in the saint's blood. This ensured that his body was given to the people for burial, and further miracles of healing ensued at his grave. Osbern also adds a cautionary note: those who tried to steal relics of the saint were miraculously stricken with illness or even killed.

In writing the *Life of Alfege* Osbern had little to draw on by way of English hagiographical tradition.[13] However he was a talented scholar and his work owes a substantial amount to the influence of classical literature. In describing the fire at Canterbury he comments: 'You would think you were looking at Nero marvelling at the flames of Rome or Aeneas weeping at the Trojan conflagration' – the details he gives of the burning of the city have something in common with Tacitus' and Virgil's descriptions of these better known fires.

Osbern clearly takes pride in his literary style, employing a number of devices to add interest and variety to his narrative. It is not simply a concatenation of miraculous events and visions, which is sometimes a tendency of hagiography. Apart from one rather abrupt jump (introducing the story of Alfege's visit to Rome) the narrative is constructed as a coherent whole told from a varied perspective. Plain narrative is interspersed effectively with direct speech, as in the vivid scene where Alfege is abandoned in the marshes. We hear his outpouring of lamentation from his own lips:

'The prison is behind me, the river in front of me, shadows are all about me and their creator is at hand!'

shortly followed by the bracing tones of the Good Angel reminding him of his duty.

At significant moments in the narrative Osbern sets the scene against the larger picture of all nature. After a sleepless and tearful night Alfege prepares to tell his monks of the vision he has had:

'And now the splendour of the sun had put the stars to flight...'

The effect of this is to highlight Alfege's address to his monks by setting it in a larger context; it adds to the momentous nature of the occasion. Intermittently Osbern breaks off from the narrative with rhetorical passages arguing the case for Alfege's sanctity. Throughout, the story unfolds on two levels: the events on earth leading up to Alfege's death, and at a higher level the machinations of the Devil thwarted by visions of saints and angels. Sometimes Osbern is a detached observer of events; at others he zooms in on the action and interjects rhetorical questions and declamation, as when he ascribes Edric's plotting to the work of the Devil:

'But the master and minister of all malice, the Devil – the Devil, I say, who is the master and minister of all malice!'

The repetition and alliteration reinforce his indignation.

Language and expression are used to striking effect in parts of the narrative. Osbern shows a liking for paradox and antithesis. The vagrants who are drawn to Alfege's community are described as 'empty of goods and full of miseries'; Alfege's persecutors are said to ' tirelessly tire him' (*indefatigabiliter fatigabant*), and there is a bold oxymoron in the description of his killer as 'moved by impious piety' (*motus impia pietate*). When the fighting between the two armies hangs in the balance, the antithetical balance of the sentence brings the message home:

'Individual Chiefs ... won frequent glorious victories over the enemy; from time to time the enemy also triumphed, not ingloriously, over them.'

A similar device is his pairing of adjective and noun, and then reversing the pair; for example, on joining the community at Deerhurst Alfege is described as:

'Inspired by the **humble severity** and **severe humility** of these people...' (*humili severitate et severa humilitate*)

The use of the ascending tricolon, frequent in classical literature, is a recurrent feature of Osbern's writing. It is often used to build up an effective crescendo, as when the Danish pirates are introduced:

'These are the most evil type of robbers on account of the fact that need makes them bold, their wandering makes them impossible to track down, and desperation makes them invincible.'

The effect of this device is redoubled in his account of the attack on Canterbury:

'Now the population was slain, now the city was burned, now indeed Christ's temple was violated, desecrated, despoiled'

where the triple group [population, city and temple] is reinforced with the repeated 'now' and topped up with the triple 'violated, desecrated, despoiled', asyndeton adding to the effect. Repetition of a word within the tricolon can serve to compound the effect, as in the description of the horror at the wound dealt to Alfege:

'The prisoners were horrified at the deed, the Danes themselves were horrified, indeed all with any humanity were horrified.'

Similarly in his description of Alfege's prison cell:

'...which the ghastliness of the gloom made foul, the cramped space made foul, the noise of the frogs made foul.'

Sometimes however the effect is rather more pedestrian with the tricolon describing simply a sequential succession of events, as with Alfege's arrival at Bath:

'When he had arrived there, he built a little hut; when built, he shut himself in it; shut in it, he lived a life of incredible rigour.'

Osbern's relish for colourful scene-painting and rhythmical repetition is evident particularly in his account of the vision Alfege receives in his cell on the evening before his death. The dank, evil-smelling prison is miraculously filled with pleasant perfume, the voices of the saints are heard and St Dunstan appears to Alfege encouraging him to be steadfast. Healed of his wounds, 'Alfege went his way, dancing with the dancers and singing with the singers.'(*Elphegus psallens cum psallentibus, exultans cum exultantibus incedit.*)

How then are we to assess Osbern's *Life of Alfege*? In our less credulous age, it may seem to have little relevance. Historians criticise its lack of hard information and 'spectacular blunders'. There seems to be some confusion about Alfege's career prior to becoming Bishop of Winchester. Osbern places him as founder of the community at Bath, but this conflicts with evidence elsewhere. Charters of 965 and 970 name Aescwig as abbot of Bath and he continued to attest charters into the mid 970s; however Alfege attests charters from 970 onwards, and is named as abbot of Bath on his appointment to Winchester in the Anglo-Saxon Chronicle. Possibly there were two abbots at Bath, or alternatively two communities. On the other hand Osbern may simply be wrong in making him the first and founding abbot. The monks at Glastonbury claimed that Alfege had been a monk and prior there before becoming Abbot of Bath, which seems plausible: Osbern then has simply missed out a stage of career. He can be criticised too for the sparse detail he gives about his time at Winchester. We know from other sources[14] that he was an active reformer of the Old Minster here, zealous in the cult of St Swithun and notable for practical achievements: he enlarged the crypt, had a new tower built and so improved the organ that 'it became one of the wonders of the world' – all of which Osbern omits.

Yet for all its defects as history, it is a compelling story. Osbern presents us with a consistent portrayal of a man entirely motivated by selfless compassion and love of God. While the particular details of Alfege's story may seem far removed from the present day, there are elements which are still sadly familiar : the seizing of hostages for ransom, torture of prisoners, the hardship of society's underclass and division within the church. In his enthronement sermon on April 19th 1991, the anniversary of St Alfege's martyrdom, Dr George Carey referred to the example of Alfege as an inspiration for the church's witness today. 'No church can or should avoid political comment when freedom, dignity and worth are threatened. The cross of Christ firmly roots us in human concerns and needs, and places us alongside the oppressed, the dispossessed, the homeless and the poor.'

Osbern's account is an assertion of values which are as relevant to the third millennium as they were at the start of the second: moral and physical courage in the face of terrible suffering, fellow feeling for all humanity and a keen sense of justice. Alfege is a saint whose memory deserves to be kept alive.

1. A large part of Osbern's life of Alfege also appears in the account by Florence (Florentius) of Worcester. Either Florence and Osbern were both using a common source, no longer extant, or Florence copied sections from Osbern.
2. The manuscript no longer exists. The full text however was one of many collected by Henry Wharton in his 'Anglia Sacra' of 1691 (vol. ii, p. 122 ff.).
3. Gibson 'Lanfranc of Bec' p. 163.
4. Osbern 'miracula S.Dunstani' cap. 17 & 19.
5. Eadmer 'de reliquiis S Audoeni', p. 367 lines 195 – 9.
6. see Alan Thacker 'Cults at Canterbury' p. 241; also Nicholas Brooks 'The Early History of the Church of Canterbury: Christ Church 597 to 1066' p. 265.
7. Eadmer describes Lanfranc as *rudis Anglus* on his arrival at Canterbury, i.e. unversed in English ways.
8. See 'The Life of St Anselm, Archbishop of Canterbury by Eadmer' edited by R W Southern, Clarendon Press (1972) p.52ff; Eadmer was born in 1060: the Life was written in early 12th century.
9. This is the inscription of the memorial tablet in the nave of St Alfege's Church, Greenwich.
10. preserved in Stubbs, 'Memorials of St Dunstan', pp. 424-5.
11. David Rollason 'The concept of sanctity in the early lives of St Dunstan'.
12. See Nicholas Brooks op.cit. p. 257, also Alan Thacker 'Deerhurst Lecture' (September 1994).
13. Alan Thacker 'Cults at Canterbury' points out that the record of the translation of Alfege's relics to Canterbury in 1023 (on which Osbern based his account of the translation of the relics) was the first work of hagiography produced at Canterbury in a long time.
14. Wulfstan 'Narratio'.

Osbern's preface to the Life of St Alfege

To all those who remain steadfast in the faith of Christ, from Osbern, unworthy son of the Holy Metropolitan Church of Canterbury. Grace be upon you, and the peace of God our Father, and Lord Jesus Christ, and the Holy Spirit.

Heaven's verdict sanctioned a heavy punishment on the man who preferred to store the money he had received in his purse rather than place it on the table of the money changers[1]. No one will find fault with me then, if I steer clear of the danger of this verdict and publish all I know about Alfege, glorious martyr of Christ, for others to know too. If I speak truly and my audience listens to advantage, providence will reward us with the bounty of its repayment so that I need not regret the hard work I put into my narration nor they the interest they pay to it.

There is another substantial reason which prompts me to speak. On the whole we lay the charge of idleness on those who knew the deeds which were done in those days to the honour of the Most High but were unwilling to pass them by the task of dictating. We certainly ought not to scold their reticence, but if we know things worthy of remembering, we ought to proclaim them. Otherwise we may blame our predecessors in this matter, yet seem far more blameworthy for that same fault to our successors.

I promise an absolutely true account of these matters. As far as its content goes, setting aside the embellishment of the words, I may declare I shall say nothing which I have not received either from eye-witnesses or those who heard it from eye-witnesses, and from people of outstanding authority and reliability. I avoid using the actual words of these people, since I do not want to disfigure the language – the 'firstfruits of speech' – with barbaric expression[2]. However I have found some accounts of these affairs written not inelegantly. From these sources I have taken the themes I judged fit to be included in this present scripture in their proper place.

Therefore relying on the help of Him through whose grace we do well whatever we do, through whose generous compassion we know whatever we know well, let us take up the Psaltery, let us play upon the Lyre! Let us make known the Martyr's everlasting glory with exultation! Let us honour his bodily Passions by imitation! We have already extolled the man in music[3] at the instigation of Archbishop Lanfranc, irrefutable Master of all Latin style. Now for the compelling reasons I have mentioned, let us extol him with our eloquence.

NOTES

1 Osbern is referring to the parable of the talents.
2 i.e. he prefers to write in Latin rather than Anglo-Saxon.
3 This is the *Hymn to St Alfege*, now lost.

Here begins the
life and passion of our
Holy Patron and Lord, Alfege,
Archbishop of Canterbury,
and Martyr

1. His early years

Originating from an illustrious family, Alfege embarked on a life of great wisdom and extreme humility. His parents marvelled at the intelligence of his mind and the innocence of his life. As if they could foretell what work divinity to was achieve through him, they handed him over to a tutor, to be imbued with learning and the wisdom of Christian religion. Both of these he embraced keenly as a young man; the latter most keenly, because it showed him Christ, and because it aroused in him a love of eternal life. When he had read and re-read all that seemed sufficient for his well being, he directed his entire study of philosophy towards loving God, desiring to know him always, to obey him, to bear his yoke. But Alfege feared that his mother's love for him stood in the way of this desire – for he was loved by his mother dearly, as no other. He prayed God earnestly to teach him how His will might be done, and how all that was most pleasing in His sight should come about, either through secret inspiration or open revelation. He promised he would omit nothing that divine goodness indicated was to be done, not through his love for his father, mother or any of his family.

So it was that touched by the spirit of majesty, heedless of his father's inheritance, and unmindful of his mother's grief, he deserted the world and entered a monastery called Deerhurst. He put on the religious habit, and in keeping with that habit so ordered his life. The place was sparsely inhabited but even so virtue ensured that those who did live there were thoroughly good people. Everything which could seduce their souls from virtue, they rejected with lively perseverance, and they were single-minded in their readiness to endure. Inspired by the humble severity and severe humility of these people, as a young man Alfege began to drive out his private desires and solitary wishes, and to be subservient to the needs of all; and to put it crudely, to make himself the instrument of all. He strove to love God with a fervent spirit tirelessly, and so that he might make as much room as possible in his life for that love, he increased this by fasting and keeping vigil with great assiduity. He would not do what was convenient to him at another's inconvenience; no, rather he would greatly seek the other's convenience to his own inconvenience. And so to sum up: he helped everybody he could, and those whom he could not help he took pains not to hinder.

2. Alfege leaves Deerhurst for Bath

Several years passed, spent in much religious duty, and the time of his youth seemed to be passing, but he made light of the tasks he had born on God's account. He strove to seize the path to a yet more austere life, and to embark on his struggle with a malignant enemy. So, he left the monastery ready to go wherever the divine grace wanted to lead him. He came to a place which is called Bath in English ('Balneum' in Latin) on account of the fact that hot water coming out from the place provides the opportunity of baths for anyone who wants to use them. When he had arrived there, he built a little hut; when built, he shut himself in it; shut in

31

it, he lived a life of incredible rigour. Without delay, Nobles flocked to him, baring the wounds of their souls and seeking heaven's will from him. They honoured him with large and generous gifts with which he was able to protect both himself and all his followers from harm of hunger and cold. Others untied the clasp of worldly ambition and set it aside. Under his teaching they came to change their life at the same time as their dress. From this it came about that in a short time a considerable group of monks was gathered there. These rejected all sensuality and guarded their souls with ways of utmost gentleness, displaying the same sincerity of their life everywhere, and maintaining the same uprightness of conduct in everything. To encourage these men in their desire for goodness, the Saint stood as such a great example, that there was no need for them to be instructed through any reading, but all might read in his life what each should avoid or imitate.

3. His teaching

He found great fault with those who changed their worldly clothing but not their life. "For if," he said "those who tell whatever lies they like are condemned by divine judgement – as the holy scripture says *the mouth which lies kills the soul*[1] – what will happen in the case of a man who hasn't a scrap of truth but who all the time offers a false appearance to all eyes? Doesn't he seem full of deceit to you, who shows himself to be what he is not? Who pretends one thing in his dress, but tells a different story in his heart? Falsehood is at work not only in the movement of one's lips, but in the display of signs. From this it follows that the intelligent man should recollect that on the day of destruction of the wicked, what great sorrow, what great confusion will encompass those whom all men now call good. On that day in the sight of all creation the sentence of everlasting vengeance will weigh down upon them. Man knows, believe me!" (this was Alfege's customary way of swearing an oath) "It is better not change one's garb than to neglect the life beneath the clothing." Yet he enjoined them to show respect to the very worst members of their faith, whether ignorant or neglectful, especially those who because of poverty or over-strict discipline had left their own Churches. Coming to English soil , empty of goods and full of miseries, they wandered here and there with no fixed abode. When a very capacious dwelling house had been completed, he imposed a rule of sobriety on his followers; he taught them to rein in their carnal desires by the harness of reason. Once a Prefect had been chosen to take the monks their food he took himself off to a very narrow cell. Cases of the most important business however were referred to him.

4. Scandalous behaviour of some of the monks

Yet in any gathering of good men life can scarcely be lived without there being a mixture of bad – at least, not until that day dawns which shows who is chosen for the fire and who for the granary. Many of his disciples paid little heed to his advice.

Forgetful of their faith and profession, they determined to embark again on the ways of the world, and plotted how they might fulfil what they had determined more opportunely. With no regard for the life of the community, in the middle of the night they ate purloined food, engaged in drunkenness and lechery, and devoted themselves to all that is dishonourable, as far as their boldness allowed; (for nobody would dare to attempt such behaviour in Father Alfege's knowledge.) But for the sake of Alfege whom they had mocked, the wrath of the Almighty was unwilling that they should go unpunished, and with terrible swift judgement struck, enveloped and slew a guilty man in his criminal act. In the night which followed the day of his burial, Alfege was celebrating the holy rites as was his custom and offering his sweet sacrifice to the Lord. He happened to hear loud voices within the vicinity of the monastery – voices of men either carrying a heavy load or straining to hold it up. Thinking either that vandals had been caught in the holy place committing sacrilege, or that the Brothers were suffering some discomfort in their sleep through the spite of Demons, he rose hurriedly and made his way to the Monastery with quickened step. When he had crossed over in front of the doors of the hall in which the monks usually ate, the shouting he had heard sounded all the clearer. The Saint halted, caught the sound in his astonished ears, and made out the words: then he burst into the building. There on the ground lay the man who had recently died, wretchedly tormented. Above him stood men of grim appearance and ghastly clothing, who were whipping him with bull-whips and fiery snakes. While he howled and let out terrible cries of pain, those who were torturing him added to his pain upbraiding him: "As you took no heed of God, so we take no heed of you." Repeating these words over and over, they dragged their prisoner from the place.

Then the Saint, broke down and burst into floods of tears. He went back wringing his hands; and as he went back, said: "O unhappy hour, when birth brought us to the light of day! How much happier we would be as brute beasts rather than be handed over to the tyranny of such tormentors after death! For when an animal dies it loses all punishment along with its life; but as long as a man lives, his labour is continuous; when he dies, if he dies in sin, his pain is everlasting." So he spoke, and spent the remainder of the night weeping and grieving without sleep.

And now the splendour of the sun had put the stars to flight, when the Saint gathered the disciples together, to tell them what he had seen and what the Lord had made evident. After they had all heard his story together, you could see some turn pale, others weep, some virtually go mad with terror, and everybody quake. When those who had been the dead man's companions in sin saw that none of their secrets was hidden from Father Alfege, they leaped into the middle and confessed their error. They begged to be punished for the evils they had done, so that they should not remain under the shadow of the divine punishment to come. On being asked where had been the usual place for their meeting and merrymaking, they showed him the very place where the spirits had tortured the soul of the dead man. Thus God in his goodness, because of a man's finest merits, would not let one man's crime lie hidden, but wanted to uncover the evils of all; he would not spare one man, but wanted to heal the ills of all.

5. A successor is sought for the Bishopric of Winchester

Meanwhile when Ethelwold Bishop of Winchester, of blessed memory, was taken from this life and brought to the heavenly kingdom, there was great dispute about who was worthy to undertake to govern the Church he had left. Different factions wanted different outcomes, but no single group was strong enough to carry their wishes through. Indeed the Clerks of that Church had adopted a thoroughly wicked way of life, living in opposition to the canon laws in every respect. Often when caught by the Priest they were unwilling to correct their depraved habits – indeed, were ready to defend what they had wickedly done with an insolent spirit. It had been decreed therefore by royal edict that they should be dismissed and that others who were more worthy should replace them in office. So when the Clerks had been driven out, Godfearing Monks were admitted. From this action, it came about that in the election for the Priesthood the Clerks wanted a Clerk and the Monks a Monk, each faction wanting someone to support their cause, and someone of their own profession in authority. How the settling of this dispute reached its conclusion not through human wit but by divine plan will later become clear.

6. Dunstan's character

At this time Dunstan, Archbishop of the Holy Church at Canterbury and in all cities in England, was presiding over the first service of the day. He was a just man in every respect, kindled with the fire of divine love beyond human reckoning. The grace of the omnipotent had so promoted and protected him, sanctified him even before his birth, that he passed all his life without any significant fault. He powerfully commanded Kings and even Tyrants with the strength of his mind and authority of his holiness. He was not the sort of man whom power could deter or favour could bribe, but he could spot injuries done to God in anyone, whether common men or Nobles, and would sharply avenge them without procrastination. No-one could ever twist him from truth and justice; no-one saw him accept a scapegoat in anyone's trial, but he meted out justice fairly to all. He neither favoured the pauper against the law, as sometimes happens, because of his poverty, nor buttered-up the rich, as men generally do because of their wealth. Thus he appeared an object of terror to the evil, but one of respect to all good men. The wars which were ended in his time are testimony to his advice and wisdom, as is the strengthened peace, the wealth of divine blessing, which poured out such a cornucopia on mortal men as no-one had seen before. Who sanctioned excellent laws, if not Dunstan? Who instituted just measures, if not Dunstan? In a word, who conferred full authority on the English Churches, if not he? When could a wicked and evil man live with him, for Dunstan could not let even good men live without discipline? In addition to this, the eloquence of his language matched the richness of his life, so that if you had seen his life of abstinence and heard his words as he preached, you would have been utterly at a loss to know what to marvel at most in the man. Thus endowed with both kinds of grace, he neither instructed others to do what he himself neglected to do, nor acted himself without knowing how to teach others.

7. Dunstan is visited by Andrew the Apostle

When it was learned that the High Priest (Archbishop Ethelwold) had gone to his rest, and that considerable disagreement of factions had arisen in the election of a priest, this blessed man feared that with such a scandal many souls would be lost to the faith. He bent his mind to the gift of prayer, in supplication to God, to whom knowledge of the future is clear. With the piety he was in the habit of showing in all situations, he asked who would be a suitable shepherd to succeed in governing the Church. While Dunstan was repeating his prayer many times over, there appeared the divine messenger, Andrew the Apostle, giving this pronouncement: "Why , dear soul, are you so sorrowful? Why do you weep, pouring out such sad lamentations? Rise, and lay your hand upon Abbot Alfege. Pour on him the holy oil, and appoint him priest of the forsaken Church. Let no other's power prevent you: this decision about him has come not from any man but from the mouth of almighty God. So that you may be in no doubt about who is talking to you, know that I am Andrew, Apostle of the son of God, and most devoted guardian of your well being." So he spoke, and as he finished speaking, disappeared. The priest was delighted by this pronouncement, and announced the message he had received from the Apostle to the ears of the council. He impressed the message on his hearers, and warned them to stop supporting their own factions.

8.   Alfege is chosen as Bishop of Winchester

A meeting was called, and all gave their opinion, shouting that they wanted what God wanted. Indeed considerable happiness gripped King Ethelred concerning two aspects: firstly that he should have in his kingdom such a monk, who was being promoted to the priesthood by divine testimony, and secondly that a priest of such merit had been found who was worthy to be considered for that promotion. The priests who had flocked to Canterbury with enthusiasm to consecrate the Priest were soon summoned. They seized Father Alfege by both his hands, escorted him to the Church, and gave out the reasons for their choice to the crowds of bystanders. There arose a great cry from the people, with praises for all the great works that God had revealed in him. "May the Bishop," they shouted, " live for countless years! May he live in God's grace; may he live showing his grace to men!" When the tumult had settled down, the priests placed on Alfege the badges of priest.[2] Next he determined to visit his own see. When this news was received, the people of Winchester – and even if they were far removed from Winchester they learned it as if by divine instruction – all led as if by one spirit, came running to meet him, shouting the words of the Benedictus: "Blessed is he that comes!" They thought that they would be fortunate indeed: if they had welcomed a man who had been sought with such great anxiety, a man revealed by so great a miracle, then they deserved to have him as a healer and protector of life. Nor were they deceived in that opinion. For from the time that the Blessed Alfege ascended the throne of the honour he had gained, he conducted himself so energetically, so effectively in all things that no-one had any doubt that he would judge them with the same compassion as the man by whose choice he had been promoted.

Therefore everywhere there was respect, everywhere reverence; no oppression of the poor, no unfair taxes of the rich. On the contrary, any man who had been particularly quick in carrying out his will was judged happy in his own opinion and that of all. Thus, free from harm the people lived freely, by listening to the word of God.

9.   Alfege's character

In Alfege, virtue increased from day to day. From his virtue, his fame grew, and from his fame came a gathering of people. So the overseers of Ecclesiastical affairs rejoiced, because they saw that the divine will had given them such a companion.

Notable bands of heroes rejoiced, since they saw that the man whom they knew to be most humanitarian in giving help would be most a welcome friend to Royalty. Alfege adapted himself to the ways of everybody, so that he was dear to everyone and no-one envied his glory – which is a rare thing among men. In him there were to be found all the qualities which befit a good and holy man, but what prompted the greatest admiration for him among the people was this: that although he showed extreme pity and kindness to everyone else, he appeared wicked and cruel to himself. This has been brought to our knowledge by those who were well acquainted with his private behaviour. In winter, when all the ground was stiff with icy cold and deep sleep held all men in its grip, he would get up secretly from his bed and make for a place outside. There, with bare feet, clad in a simple robe, he would stand for a long time in prayer, until the rising Sun put the lesser stars to flight and he himself realised the presence of the Sun. He would go inside as if to take food, but would get up from the table almost as empty as when he had come to the table: he ate just enough for his friends to refute that he had not eaten at all. His body was made so thin by this fasting, that at the time of the Holy Sacrament, when he was stretching his hands held on high in the Ecclesiastical manner, daylight could be seen right through the middle of his joined hands, if he happened to be standing in front of a window through which the sun's ray was pouring brightly. This was seen by a number of people on more than one occasion.

10. His generosity

What great strength of pity and generosity shone in that man is, I think, beyond the power of human mind to guess at or tongue to explain. He knew how to adapt his speech and mind to every kind of person. To explain this point, it will be a sufficient indication that he did not allow any of his parishioners ever to beg in public, nor did he let any poor man from another district go away empty. He thought it a great and terrible wrong if any man should want to keep for his private property what nature produced for the common good. Consequently he would argue earnestly that anyone who was not willing to help someone in need was not a member of the Lord's body. For while one part of a body suffers, the whole body suffers with it: it is evident therefore that something is not a part of the same body which, when another part is suffering, does not know how to have any feeling of compassion. Those who ought to outdo the enemies of Christ in this quality of compassion, are actually outdone by them: not only are they outdone, but in being outdone they expose themselves to derision, which is a blasphemy against Christ. "Look at the Jew, and consider the Heathen!" he said. "Observe with what great love they are bound to each other for the sake of preserving their religion. You will see that among them no-one labours for want of family property: they would be eager to relieve any such man by pouring money on him. While these men see us deficient in that virtue, to which they are drawn by natural affection, they are in truth being instructed through divine teaching. With a blasphemous mouth they attack Christ, the faith and religion of Christians, the expectation of bliss to come. So on whom does that blasphemy chiefly reflect, if not those who disdain to help the poor and feel compassion?" With such sermons the possessors of riches were stirred to almsgiving just as the spirit to fight in battle is roused by the clangour of trumpets. Consequently, nobody remained in need in that county, but the Blessed Alfege helped all, both through his own efforts, through the powerful men of his day, and certainly through the relations of those who were in need. Then when those supplies ran out with which by Church law he could help the poor, he ordered the Church's treasures, which he himself had multiplied, to be distributed. He directed that all the most elaborate items the Churches possessed, which were an honour in times of good fortune, were to be used in times of need.

Therefore, as we have said, this man who was all honesty, had loathing for himself, and the greatest loving regard for others.

11. Alfege becomes Archbishop of Canterbury

There is no point in speaking about the miracles done by him while he was bishop, for two reasons. Firstly he possessed the virtues through which those who have been able to perform miracles have shone, and secondly our main purpose is to relate what we have been able to find out from genuine sources about his glorious martyrdom. This we shall do, in turn, once we have said a few words about his time as Patriarch.

When Dunstan, defender of justice, heard the rumour how Alfege was spoken of as great and admirable amongst the people, he poured out lofty praises to almighty God, who had shed such great light on his home shores in his lifetime. But he knew that his merits – or rather the gifts of God – deserved to be crowned soon, and he feared that God's church was being thrown in turmoil by a succession of evil-doers. He assailed the ears of divine mercy with his anxious pleadings, asking how he might leave Alfege as heir to his Patriarchy. As soon as his prayer was heard, what he asked for was promised to him; though what had been promised was fulfilled not at once but in the course of time. I think that the reason the matter was put off was so that it might be clear to all how much God loved Dunstan, since he so kindly made him a promise in his lifetime and fulfilled it truthfully long after he was dead. Another reason was so that that day would come to find Alfege which could bring him to a martyr's glory. For when the fifth year in which both Dunstan and Alfege been Pontiffs was over, Dunstan, with a great gathering of Angels entered into the Lord's bliss, and there were three successors after him to the Patriarchy. When these had happily come to the last judgement to take their places with their fathers, all the English priests met in turn with all the Senatorial order, to decide in joint discussion who ought to be in charge of all. Everybody raised the name of Alfege, all magnified Alfege with one voice, vied with each other to raise their hands for Alfege. So in the

1006th year of the incarnation of Divinity, in the fourth quarter, in the 578th year since the arrival of the Angles to Britain, Alfege was translated from Winchester to Canterbury, elevated to Archbishop, at the age of 52. He had earned this through his long exercise of ecclesiastical discipline, filled as he was with all possible human grace.

What grief then, what murmuring assailed the people of Winchester! I cannot say, nor can anyone other than those who saw the people of Canterbury cheering him, for the greatness of Canterbury's joy was an indication of Winchester's great gloom. The former were just as delighted to receive Father Alfege as the latter were to lose him.

12. En route for Rome, he is attacked and robbed in Ausonia

When a few days had passed, which he spent in sorting the details of his as yet unfamiliar position, he arranged to go to the Eternal City. On arrival at Ausonia[3], he entered the first town he came across. Worn out with the extent of journey, he was resting. The townsfolk, not knowing who he was, thinking only of their own greed, burst into his house. They ransacked his belongings, and with both words and blows forced the Saint to leave, robbed of his goods. He bore their ill-treatment lightly, grieving only moderately for his goods, and made his way back on the road by which he had come. He had not gone far from the town, when astonishingly ghastly firebrands seized the walls of the town, threatening to make ash of the buildings, and destruction to the citizens. Roused by the fire, the people left their beds and ran headlong everywhere with frenzied step. The flame grew to a vast size and spread everywhere, and there was no hope among the citizens of avoiding it. Moved by a saner realisation of what they had done, his assailants went over the matter in their minds just in case the fire should be blazing to avenge him. Going out with the notables of the place, they looked for the man, found him, begged and pleaded with him. Alfege, always most tender hearted, said "Let us go back so that we may see the fire from close by." Standing there the Priest looked at the fire, shed tears and called on God. O power of the Creator! O mercy of the Saviour! Alfege wept, and he moved the fire. The people applauded. Immediately the fire hung suspended in the air; it crossed through countless houses and was discovered outside the town walls. All reasonably intelligent people who woke up to the contemplation of what had happened prided themselves that Angels had intervened to save them. But when the author of the miracle was made known, all the crowd rushed through the gates like water through cracks, to say their prayers and to offer gifts. Saint Alfege replied to them: "Please keep what is yours, my own goods are enough for me. Nevertheless, from now on you will not turn any stranger from your doors. Instead you will undertake to look after all, and take care to look after those duties you have undertaken. For God lives in all good men, and for that reason you should be glad to welcome any man and so welcome God." So saying he took back his belongings and instructed the crowd to go back with theirs.

13. Alfege arrives at Rome: he meets the Pope, and has a premonition of the death of the Bishop of Winchester

Finally arriving at Rome, he announced his presence to the Roman Pontiff, and sought an audience. The Pope took every opportunity to speak to him. During their conversation they were bound to each other with such affection that the Pope wrapped his own Apostle's stole around him. He honoured him in the presence of all the Roman Senate in the memory of Saint Peter, the keeper of the keys of heaven. While this was happening and they spent the days talking to each other, on one of the days a serious sadness overcame Alfege. This caused him to abandon his usual manner and disposed him to behave quite unlike his usual self. His companions were puzzled by his uncharacteristic behaviour and approached him in turn. Artfully they tried to discover the reasons for his sorrow, and to relieve his mind through sensitive consolation. But continuing in the gloomy mood of his depression, he said: "No-one will see me in good spirits today, since the man who succeeded me as Bishop of Winchester[4] has died." It was not easy for them to believe him, on account of the fact that nobody had arrived to bring news of the event. Yet there again it was hard for them to disbelieve him, since they knew that God was in the man and did not believe that he could tell a lie about the matter. They noted what day it was, to see whether he had foretold that event through prophetic utterance or hazarding a guess. Then, when the Pope and Archbishop had exchanged greetings with one another, they started the journey back, with mixed feelings. Returning on foot, Alfege had now come over the Alps, when a number of English nobles ran to meet him. These had been chosen either for their enthusiasm for prayer or desire for sight-seeing, and were trying to reach the City of Rome. When they were asked about the Bishop, already now lamented by God's servant Alfege, they said that the man had departed life on that very day when Alfege had begun to weep. What divine grace shone in the heart of this Blessed man! What could surpass it? He knew what stirred in his own land though he was far away. He knew that the soul of the Bishop of Winchester had left its fleshly habitation while still he dwelt at Rome as a traveller. The fame of this deed spread far and wide through the land, and persuaded men to think about him much more than can be thought of about a man, since he could so easily know and so truly tell what happened far away.

14. He returns to Britain: his conduct of services

But let us return to the man himself, at the point where we left off. On landing in Britain, placed on the throne of the Fathers, not only did he not diminish his former standing, but he increased it incomparably. From that time on he never failed to hold Councils frequently and opportunely, or to expound the orthodox faith to the Fathers. He ensured that those who ought to remove the errors of others should not themselves be in error, and wander deviating from the path of truth. If he could not turn sinners to God through his words, then he did so by acts of kindness. He neglected nothing that was in their interest, until those whom his words of admonition would not correct were won over by the generosity of his kindness. He himself wept for the sins of all, and offered the saving sacrifice for the good of all every day. If a special Solemn Feast day fell due, on which it was appropriate for him as priest to offer thanks on behalf of the people, led by the hands of the priests into the Sanctuary, he kept himself apart. During the hymns which were sung with all the noise of festivity, he would conduct Mass privately, in a manner all the more reverent as he was further from the gaze of the people. Then filled with God, on returning to the altar he would go through the service which he had begun before. He would spend the day clad in a white robe with the pall on top, his hair bound back, so that through the external habit of his clothing he might rouse the internal habit of virtue. His purpose also was that all those who saw him might become the more devoted to reverence, just as they saw him more fitted for grace.

While he sat as governor of the Church, under Christ, he endowed the Church with many outstanding treasures. Afterwards, either Alfege himself spent this for the use of the poor, or else the heathen had carried it off in loot for their own improper uses. The virtue of modesty held first place in him to such an extent that nobody dared to let out an obscene word in his hearing or carry out a shameful deed in his sight. He used to say that this was the first and chief rule in preserving chastity, as modesty, the handmaid of manners, curbs those whom boldness, the corrupter of souls, spurs on.

But why should I say more about his goodness? Even the most accomplished eloquence is inadequate for the telling of his kind heartedness. He entirely streamed with mercy, he entirely melted in tears. He was the most loving consoler of the poor, generous in giving, reluctant to receive. He was the one hope to all the afflicted who came to him, the one refuge for the afflicted in this land. So it came about that he did not shrink from giving all that there was, until nothing of his remained which he could bestow on his neighbours. He would rather lose this life and die, than live and not benefit his neighbours.

15. The Danish pirates Swan and Thyrkill attack Britain

During this same period of time, there were pirates. These are the most evil type of robbers on account of the fact that need makes them bold, their wandering makes them impossible to track down, and their desperation makes them invincible. Under the leadership of Swan and Thyrkill, strongest Chiefs of the Danes, they brought many a blight to English land. When Swan was killed in a terrible manner by almighty God, Thyrkill gained the leadership of his evil inheritance. With him at their head, the pirates wandered into all the harbours of the sea, leaping out of their boats now here, now there. They tended to cause great loss amongst those that lived nearby rather than inspiring terror amongst those living further off. That type of enemy was not the sort to respect goodness, or to be sparing in the face of anyone's loyalty. The only good thing about them was that they were not willing to make a pledge and then break it – and that was so only from time to time. Amongst them there was no respect for God; or if they had any respect, they had no sense of religious duty. They treated all the days of the year the same; they ate all foods just the same. Not only did they not receive the rites of the holy mysteries, but they did not even enter the church. Also, they despised legitimate marriages: the more closely related someone was, the more pleasing the union was. Since they made no pretence of religion in anything they did, their goodness waned and cruelty waxed from day to day. It was as if it were law that each man would set the limit to his evil doing just where his capacity for it failed. So when any obstacle gave way, the enemy was scattered throughout England. They attacked whatever stood in their way with both slaughter and arson. When the coastal region had been deserted by the inhabitants, there was an influx of refugees from all directions to the nearby cities. The land lay at the mercy of the raiders' fury, not blessed with any cultivation. For Ethelred, king of the English, was as weak as he was unwarlike, in his conduct more like a monk than a soldier. Men corrupted by wealth, gripped by desires, thought nothing worthwhile except their physical comfort. Consequently, to speak of military service, to do anything bravely, to be willing to die for one's country so that no-one might infringe a man's rights on his death and seize what he had prepared for himself – all this they thought utterly stupid and execrable. Thus while each man feared for himself and his property, all refrained from war as such; no-one attempted to take part in a struggle for the sake of all. The struggle was more of the kind that each man would fight as brilliantly as possible only for what he personally wanted. Individual Chiefs however, each protecting their own regions with as much strength as they could, won frequent glorious victories over the enemy; from time to time the enemy also triumphed, not ingloriously, over them.

16. Alfege acts as a mediator between Danes and English

In this great crisis Alfege used to approach the enemy – something which was actually very difficult. He would bring them the gospel word of life, pay a ransom and redeem prisoners, and feed those who were oppressed by hunger. Divine grace enabled him to find favour with the enemy to such an extent that not only did he free the prisoners from their captivity in this world, but also their captors from their eternal captivity in the next. He summoned to the faith those who had not experienced it, and invited those who had joined the faith to show their faith in action. But although the majority of the population – a great throng– had been added to the number of believers, still a considerable number were held back by the error of their disbelief. They envied their companions' well-being, and in an unspeakable conspiracy made plans to kill the author of that well-being. They were afraid that if those on whose help they relied in war were taken away, they would have less opportunity to attack and less power to resist when the occasion demanded. Consequently, the more Alfege was respected, revered and loved by the faithful, the more he was despised, mocked and ultimately killed by the faithless. But that Blessed man preferred to stand with the Lord and be called Beezlebub rather than stand with the Pharisee and be called Rabbi. He did not cease to work at the task he had begun, to comfort the faithful in the faith, to call the faithless to the faith, and to do everything with the highest authority. It would hardly have been right for him to give way to terror of others, when he had the divine spirit to govern his mind and the majority of the people to support his will.

17. The Devil plans Alfege's downfall

But the master and minister of all malice, the Devil – the Devil, I say, who is the master and minister of all malice! – could not impel the faithless few to the unjust slaughter of that just man, because of the abundance of the faithful. And so the Devil embarked on another means accomplishing the evil deed. By this means those men who had lost all fear of their companions most cruelly achieved the goal which they had most wickedly plotted. For the king had placed one Edric as Prefect of all his kingdom. He was really a man of low birth, but one whose tongue had acquired wealth and nobility for him. Brilliant in wit, smooth in eloquence, he had surpassed all men of that time in envy and treachery, as well as in arrogance and cruelty. His brother firstly gratuitously slandered the nobility of Canterbury in the presence of the King, then seized by forcible constraint those goods which had come to both him and his brother from their father's inheritance. As I say, Edric's brother was a deceitful and proud man, and had attacked the Nobles. The same Nobles had then killed him and had set fire to his house. God's just judgement ensured that the man who had unjustly set fires against others should himself pay the penalty of a just vengeance. His surviving brother raged for blood and demanded revenge of the king. The King refused his demand, and announced that his brother had been killed with justice, since he had presumed to make an attack on such great nobles with such fickleness of spirit in the Royal Palace. Changing colour, the Prefect left the palace. He gathered ten thousand men, as well-armed as possible, and tried to avenge his brother's death. In his attempt he noticed his men had advanced only little, while men whom he considered the most unfit enemies were resisting and fighting back with great courage. Provoked to anger, he sought out the Danes' encampment and asked for help, no longer just to fight against the men of Canterbury, but to invade the territory of all Britain. With curses he complained about their cowardice, saying that they had done nothing for so many years. They were wasting away, the King[5] especially, with old age and weariness, the Chiefs with leisure, and all of them with wealth and pleasure. All that was needed was to make a start: the rest would follow of its own accord. After the victory, the kingdom was to be divided equally: he would rule the English in the south while they would gain the north. The leaders of the Danes were roused by this man's promises, and at the same time they thought of their companions taken from them by the teaching of the Archbishop, Alfege. They promised that they would be tireless companions in whatever enterprise he wanted, and both parties shook hands and swore an oath on it.

18. The Danes and Edric's army combine forces

So it was that a pact was made between the Dane and the English. The Danes abandoned the post they had begun for the sake of spending the winter close to London, and with a fleet of well-armed ships too numerous to count came right up to the port of Sandwich. No doubt this was because they understood it was big enough to accommodate their ships, as well as very close to the city to which they were heading. Edric met them with a vast crowd of foot-soldiers. He himself was an infantryman, and had amassed an irresistible army. All were bent on slaughter at Canterbury: the Danish enemy to kill the Priest, the Prefect to kill the Nobles. The town of Canterbury was strongly disturbed by the rumour of this, because there were insufficient supplies of food in the town, nor was there sufficient time for making preparations now. They placed all their hopes and fortunes into the hands of the highest Priest. God's temple, which was respected with most commendable reverence from all the population, was thronged with frequent pleas for mercy. They thought that they could find protection there because of the sanctity of the place. Anything was more likely, they thought, than that they would be forcibly turned out of such a place by the hand of the enemy. But the true and everlasting God is not as the gods of the heathen. They not only grant freedom to sin to their followers, but even induce these men to sin by their very rites and rituals. They fear that men deny the honours owed to them if they do not seek to please them by the deadly permissiveness of shameful pleasures. This is what the idolatrous fictions of Comedies came from. This is how Drama Festivals came to be inaugurated, and all the other things evil Demons have devised for souls – adulterous and illiberal Gods, who clearly have no regard for their worshippers if they have not granted men freedom from sin. But all-powerful God, our Lord, does not show himself in need of any of our goods, and thus proves that he is a true God. The worship he demands means he has no fear of giving men precepts for living; he gives precepts for living so that he may extend rewards to those that obey him but punishment for those that despise him. And something that the foolish think is even harsher: those whom he loves more dearly than the rest, their sins he punishes more heavily. Hence when David had promised that the kingdom was to be strengthened, he bound his descendants with these words:[6] "If they break my statutes and keep not my commandments; Then will I visit their transgression with the rod, and their iniquity with stripes; Nevertheless my loving-kindness will I not take utterly from him." Thus those who appear to be deserted like this are by no means actually deserted by God in his Goodness.

19. The nobles beg Alfege to flee, but he refuses

Soon all the Nobles who had once taken vengeance on the violator of the law, all the Nobles I say, surrounded the Pontiff with tearful lamentation and begged him to leave the city. His life was worth more than the lives of all in the land. The Blessed Alfege felt that their coaxing, though well-meant was nevertheless unworthy of his consideration. "I must journey far, I think, on a different road," he said. "Reflecting on the tasks that lie before me, I ponder the eternal retribution of God. You seem to be giving me this sort of advice: that I should count for nothing all I have held dear in life, and that I should cast away of my own accord something which I always sought from God with all my heart, something which he has offered. There is no way that I would exchange my glory for disgrace, that through fear of death I would shun immortality, which has been offered to all by God. If immortality could be attained by any means, whether disgraceful or honourable, then we should have to strive with all our might to attain it somehow. Yet as it is, there is such great honour in dying for it, that the man who is willing to lose his life is more praiseworthy than the man who strives to save it. So who would not rush to meet death of his own accord if those who love him most dearly want to keep him from death? I have not committed the sins of wicked men, so as to fear death's punishment on these grounds. Or will this charge be brought against me: that I have drawn away their elect from their Pagan errors, and brought them to recognition and worship of the one true God? If chance brings me to die in such a cause, for which all Christ's martyrs laboured to die, I am blessed. Or perhaps this is what I have done wrong: I have restored to freedom those of our people who were prisoners, and those whom I was not able to restore to freedom I did not hesitate to feed in their captivity? Then let as many mortal wounds rain down upon me as nature has given me limbs. Indeed the immensity of their rage has blazed up against me because everyday I have reproved their life, riddled with wrongs and wickedness as it is. But it is God's authority which has compelled me, who says the blood of the wicked is to be sought from me, if the wrongdoer's wickedness is not made known to him. I should certainly be a hired hand rather than a good shepherd if on seeing my sheep devoured by the wolf I begin to contemplate my own escape. God has inspired some men to be willing to endure good and ill side by side: let them expect whatever of both kinds has been prepared for us here."

After they heard these words a council was soon called. The men preferred anything to death and torture, and all went their separate ways. Most acceded for the sake of placating the Danes. They thought that they would be safe amongst the enemy, since they could not be safe within the walls of the city. However it turned out to be quite the opposite. I am disgusted to relate what happened. When the poor of his people had been called together, Alfege encouraged them to be of good courage, to keep God before their eyes, to have no fear save of him who can destroy body and soul in the pit. He reminded them too of Christ's humility and endurance. For though he was God, and the Father had freely given him all things, he refused to take vengeance on his enemies. Not only this, but he even forbade Peter's love for him in its fury from taking revenge, and buried his sword, stained with Malchus'[7] blood, in its scabbard. He taught that there are two ways of freedom for men, one of which the public approves, the other hidden. If the best outcome in men's opinion does not turn out, they should not worry too much. In support of these words, he put before them the steadfastness and the triumphs of the Martyrs, who showed their faith not with words but with the torments they endured. Christian innocence was not so much an honour for them as a punishment, as long as they lived. The Blessed Alfege ensured that steeped in these words of his they were prepared for whatever torments the persecutor would fling at them. Then after pouring out his blessing upon them, when the communion had been poured in the holy kiss of peace, while all were sharing in the holy banquet, he commended himself to them, and them to him, and both to God the protector of all.

20. The siege and destruction of Canterbury

And now came the day that was to see the first disturbances. The whole city, surrounded by the enemy army, denied all freedom for the citizens to go out. Those standing in front of the walls were not so much displaying the courage to resist as feigning it. Yet on the twentieth day of the siege,

59

when all that they had prepared for life had been exhausted, a man was sent from the Archbishop to make a proposal to the Danes. He said they should desist from what they had begun. The people were enduring the siege innocently. They should beware of abusing insolently the rod of divine correction which God has given for the timely chastisement of his sons: it generally happens that when a father beats his heir with the stick, the stick is later thrown on the fire.

But the English had turned more inclined towards impiety the more they saw their own people being afflicted. They pressed upon them all the more fiercely, brought siege-mantlets, built siege towers, battered the wall with rams, hurled blazing torches and left nothing untouched. Then wildly through adjoining houses the fire took hold, raised its terrifying plumes and with the raging south-west wind scattered itself spreading through the entire region. You would think you were looking at Nero marvelling at the fire of Rome or Aeneas weeping at the fire of Troy. Then indeed there was a pitiful delay amongst the citizens as they considered whether they should desert the defences of the walls and fly to their own homes. The common good lost out to private suffering, the sweet recollection of their sons, the innate impulse to protect their family. And so they ran headlong in their rage, daring in their desperation, not thinking of life, not willing to die. They snatched their wives and dear children from the midst of the flames, only to be struck at once by the enemy's sword. But while they were too busily occupied with the ashes of the buildings, – and this is too pitiful to relate! – the city was broken open and the army entered. A terrible sound went up from the clamour of voices and the clangour of trumpets together, to such an extent that the all the foundations of the city appeared to be shaken to the core.

What scenes there were then, how pitiable the confusion of troubles, can come within the knowledge of no-one who was not there to see the disaster. Some were pierced by the sword, others devoured by the flames, yet more fell headlong from the walls. Several, shameful to say, hanged themselves through fear and so died. Mothers whose noble birth distinguished them from the rest were compelled to produce treasure which they did not have. They were dragged by the hair through all the city squares, and at last were thrown on the flames and died. Worst of all their cruelty raged against the young. Babies were snatched from their mother's breast and caught on spears, or were crushed as a cart was driven over them. As for the evils that followed, I can scarcely relate them because of the greatness of my grief. The revered Priest could not endure such terrible devastation of his people. By chance he had been surrounded in the Church of the Saviour by a crowd of wailing monks, but suddenly he slipped out of the grasp of those holding him and escaped from the Church. Running to a place packed with corpses, he planted himself in the thick of the enemy, groaning and crying out: "Spare us, spare us; and if you know you are men, stop persecuting innocent youngsters. It is no victory, when innocent babes and sucklings are destroyed. Waging war on suppliants will not be counted praiseworthy, whatever is achieved. If you seek glory from victory, cutting the throat of him whom heavenly power has decided to put in charge of all will offer you this most of all. Come, take me! To increase the Christian population I have robbed you of a great army! I have always condemned you freely for your impiety! I have fed, clothed, ransomed many prisoners of the land in the horrifying prison! If evil men delight in what is freely offered, your anger should rage chiefly against me, against one who above all, I agree, has offended you in so many ways." Immediately that bravest of God's athletes was grabbed by countless hands. His words were cut short even as he spoke, as he was throttled. His hands were shackled with chains, his cheeks were scratched with nails; his sides were bruised with fists and feet. In the midst of all this God's servant remained mute, and did not betray his pain by so much as a word. Fortified by the consolation of the Holy Spirit he just moved his lips slightly as if speaking with God. Thus led – or rather, pushed by impious hands – to the hall of the temple, he was commanded to stand there, spectator of a new crime. This was so that he might see death before his own death, and so there could be no kind of death which passed him by without him either enduring it or condoling with his friends. So those sons of the Devil assailed the temple of the son of all-powerful God. They set fire to barrels which had been stacked there; then they burned the roof. Now the lead melted by the fire began to trickle down. The blessed group of Monks, their heads covered by their cloaks, their faces wet with bitter tears, placed all their trust in God and came out, to give up for the Saviour what he thought worthy to lay down for all. To kill them by the sword, the cruel executioner came hurrying to meet them, and hacked them down in remarkable and relentless slaughter. What then, I ask, was going through the mind of the Priest? When he saw the mother church of all the kingdom lying enveloped in pitiful ashes, numerous piles of her sons dying by diverse devastation of diverse deaths; himself ensnared in chains, assailed with wounds, heaped with insults, bereft of consolation? Each singly would have been calamity enough to the kingdom – either the harm done to the Priest or the deadly destruction of the city – so that deprived of either glory England would never from that time on regain her former status. Whatever it is that divine wisdom intended in this deed, something great and glorious can be discerned. For the Archbishop was honoured with so good, so outstanding a Martyrdom: good in the grief he showed for the death of his sons, outstanding in that he took death upon himself.

21. The decimation of the population of Canterbury

Of all that number, which came to about eight thousand men, we learn that there remained only four of the profession of Monk, but eight hundred men of lesser rank. Firstly the men were counted out with every tenth man spared, then they were severely flogged; finally they either judged them worth putting up for ransom or took them away with them to be sold for slaves. I think that the only reason the Danes spared them was so that in future times there would still be men to speak of their bloody victory. But God makes good use of men's evil: what they intended as evidence of their cruelty he was planning for the restoration of posterity.

22. The imprisonment of Alfege

Up till now, we have wept for the destruction of the city; now let us summon our tears to weep for the death of the Saint. Now the population was slain, now the city was burned, now indeed Christ's temple was violated, desecrated, despoiled. The Saint was dragged out, his body all in chains, to be killed at the hands of the raging mass. When he was being dragged to the North gate, with those in front pulling him, and those behind pushing, those who, as I mentioned a little earlier, were the sole survivors of the whole collapse of the city, were being held under military guard, their feet strapped to boards. When they saw the Archbishop and what they were doing to him, they held up their hands to heaven at the injustice of the evil, and called out with a great moan, demanding that God should gaze on this great cruelty. For all the prisoners saw him, and raised their voices and wept. However, as he stopped to strengthen their broken spirits by his speech, the highest priest was suddenly wounded by a heavy blow on his shoulders from those who were pushing him A stream of blood flowed out and his shoulder appeared to be severed from his whole body. The prisoners were horrified at the deed, the Danes themselves were horrified, indeed all with any humanity were horrified. Yet he did not falter in praying to God. Tirelessly he fixed his gaze on the heavens and his mind on him who him who is above the heavens. He was led, a hostage for Christ, from the city to the Danish fleet, from the fleet to the jail, and from the jail to the court. I speak now of the jail, which the ghastliness of the gloom made foul, the cramped space made foul, the noise of the frogs made foul. There they kept this man of God incarcerated under guard for seven months, as they thought he would rob the Church of its wealth and give it to them for his freedom. But Alfege clearly never thought of this at all, for it seemed madness to him to enjoy this mortal life yet be cut off from the eternal presence of God. Therefore he endured all things most patiently, he celebrated Christ's sufferings as far as he could in that place, and gave thanks to God with a contrite heart.

23. Illness attacks the enemy – Alfege cures them with bread he has blessed

Meanwhile the wrath of almighty God began so to rage against the murderous people, that in a short space of time two thousand of them were stricken dead with terrible suffering of their internal organs, and the remaining masses struck by a similar disease were verging on a similar death. They were advised by the faithful to turn to Christ, to recognise his temple and his people, to speak, to weep and show remorse about everything to the Priest. They took a different view of this plan for their safety, however, thinking that this ill circumstance had happened to them not so much from divine will as from bad luck. Meanwhile the disaster imposed itself on all flesh, and with now ten, now twenty, now more seized by this terrible stomach pain, racked, and consumed, it struck those yet living with great terror of death. A plan was made and soon they all ran to Alfege; they wept for their crime with albeit unwilling tears; they begged him to make a supplication to the King of heaven. Then came that solemn day of reconciliation, on which the Saviour entrusted the most holy mystery of his body and his blood to his disciples.[8] Then Alfege, whom the malice of the torturers was fiercely tormenting only a little beforehand, was led in honour escorted by the hands of those same men before the public view of the masses. Placed on a chair, he uttered these words from his holy heart. "Even if your incessant cruelty left no room for pardon, it would still be our duty to consider not so much what you ought to suffer as what we ought to do. We have the greatest proof of this in the action of Christ the Lord. When he thought it right to wash his disciples' feet, he did not leave out the man by whom he foretold he was to be betrayed: he even fed him with Holy bread, offered by his most holy hands.

"And this is an indication of his great goodness: those whom he sees resisting the edicts of heaven with a stubborn spirit, he yet allows to live. Indeed he even permits them outstrip others in human prosperity, as long as both the mercy of heaven and the abundance of the earth, the grace of their sons, the service of their household, the increase of their wealth and the subjection of their enemies smiles upon them. This much he grants to you men also – I call you men indeed, though you always live like dogs. He extends his long patience: he would have cut you off with the sword of his fury, had he not preferred your repentance to your death. Since I desire to live in imitation of his examples, I shall forget the burning of the city, forget the impious deeds done against me, forget the slaughter of the innocent. Just as he himself prayed to his father for those who put him on the cross, so I shall intercede for my torturers. Bring bread, so that it may be returned to you straightaway as the means of your well-being. When you have fed on this and gained the goodness of the health you have wished for, you may either give solemn thanks to the Saviour or else continue blasphemers, in even greater wickedness." After the Protector finished speaking, calling on Christ as the creator of the world, he gave everyone bread that had been blessed by him, and so freed them all from the deadly plague.

24. The Danes persist in holding Alfege prisoner and asking a ransom

These people were freed and comforted by the man; all the same they persisted in the plan they had settled on. However they waited for the Sabbath, the day sacred to the Lord's rest. When they observed that they had recovered their health completely, and that of all their people not one had died throughout the whole three day period, the Chiefs of the Danish legions chose four men. These were firstly to approach the Priest and thank him for the kindness he had done them, then to put before him the substance of these terms: that if he wanted to obtain his life and liberty, he should pay sixty talents of silver, weighed in single talents of fifty pounds. In addition to this he was to promise that he would persuade the King that two hundreds talents of greater weight should be paid, since it was impossible for the English to make peace with the Danes without a large sum of money. Thus the treaty between the two peoples would be firmly established. When he had received this message, he is said to have given the following reply. "The deputation is not a legitimate one, since what is sought is something which can justly be denied to the seeker. It can be denied with justice, because it cannot be reasonably considered. It cannot be reasonably considered, because either fire has consumed the money or looting has carried it off. But if you are led to satiate the greed which masters your soul by reasoning that I would either purloin the treasures of the Church or persuade the King against the honour of our country, you are deceived. It is not the act of a Christian man to give the flesh of Christians to Pagan teeth for them to chew. Indeed this is what I should be doing, if I were to hand over what poverty had set aside to save life simply for you to devour."

However, men with whom he had been on friendly terms came to him and asked him to speak less harshly, and to authenticate a document with his seal. This document was to be sent around for seizing the Church's goods so that the price of the ransom could be gathered together from this source. But Alfege, ever a Father of the poor and unconquered defender of his Country, was annoyed that they should put dishonourable proposals to him and made the following reply. "If you could persuade me to commit that crime, you could persuade to commit any crime. For what more unworthy thing could be said than that Alfege learned to be cruel in his old age? Alfege, whom the virtue of mercy and gentleness adorned from his childhood cradle? What thanks in return shall I hope for from God, who is the most just rewarder of all, if things which have been gathered for the honour of the Church by the toil of the faithful are scattered and perish through my doing? Have you forgotten how the Most Blessed Martyr Lawrence, with excellent reasoning, hid the treasures of the Church so that his persecutor's violent hand should not find it? If he nobly hid those treasures which he had received, shall I cruelly demand treasures which I have not received, and shall I yet more cruelly hand them over? He gave the needy what they did not have: shall I snatch from those same needy what little they have? You must see that what you thought you had said with good sense was in fact an impious suggestion." This was what he said to them: they had nothing to reply.

But once what he had said was heard throughout the Danish camp, they breathed the poison of their fury against him. They gnashed their teeth, and shouted. With malicious mind they plotted what was to be done about the man. The starvation he had already undergone counted for nothing, his chains – for nothing, the soldiers' custody of him– nothing. New torments were devised and heaped upon him, multiplied by his tormentors. His was a pitiful condition, which not only dumb animals but even sticks and stones would blanch at. Until Easter, the day on which all the corners of the earth rejoiced in the resurrection of the Creator, he was being punished by the secret inquisitions of his tormentors. But Alfege had hope in the Lord, and rejoiced in all these evils as if at a feast.

25. The devil tempts Alfege, taking him out of prison

So it was that the spiteful fury of the impious Dragon raged against him. Satan believed that he himself would die by the dread dagger of envy if Alfege whom he could not defeat by the torments of his soldiers did not give in, defeated by Satan's own arts. He covered the force of his rage with the cloak of piety; he tried to him trip up by deceit since he could not overpower him with the magnitude of his terror. He was Virtue in disguise – but not in deed. He became an Angel in his face, but not in fact.

When the fifth day of the Easter feast was over, the author of darkness approached the son of light. He lied, saying that he had come from the heavens above, to soothe the watchmen into a gentle sleep, and that he would lead him from the filth of the prison to safety for the good of the people. He should not be afraid to branded with the reputation of a cowardly soldier: for he was not more lofty than Peter, nor tougher than Paul. A basket had protected the latter, and an Angel had freed the former when he was weighed down by the noise of the prison. Christ too turned honourably away and went out of the temple to escape from the hands of those throwing stones, and in his gospel he gave his disciples permission to flee. Steeped in these words as if in perfumes, Alfege left the prison, following on his journey the leader who presumed to tempt the son of God in the desert. But when they had crossed the marshes through the dark shadows of night, the one who was playing the part of the Good angel suddenly disappeared. Then the Saint realised the trickery of his pestilential guide. He sighed out his grief from the depths of his heart, threw himself down in the middle of the marshes and called upon his Saviour with great weeping. "O giver of life, o only protector of Adam's line, why has your grace deserted me in my old age when it never failed me in my vigorous youth? Did you save me so mercifully, only to cast me away and let me perish at the end of my life? O all that I long for, all I desire to enjoy, what good is it to be victorious in the battle through the long day, if when the day is done, the conquered makes off with the conqueror as his battle prize? What praise is there in being skilled at swimming, if the shipwrecked sailor escapes the middle of the ocean, but meets the shipwreck of an unseen death on the shore? How often have I found you a Saviour in the shipwreck of this life? Now I shall try to find a comforter in this illusion of the Devil, a helper in chance and adversity. I say a helper in adversity: I shall find you a consolation; I shall find you a consolation in this deceit of the Devil. The prison is behind me, the river in front of me, shadows are all about me and their creator is at hand." Alfege thus surrounded cried out: "You were the only refuge of the poor: you will be a helper to your pupil!"

26. The Good Angel guides him back

So he cried out, no longer resplendent in his priesthood but bowed with shame. His voice racked with groaning, he did not cease to pour his lamentations into God's ears. But God who created a column of light in the midst of darkness for his chosen people to find the path in the wilderness, thought it right now to show him a path in his wandering. By this route the noble champion might return to the place from which he had come, and without further hindrance earn the promised crown of heaven. Soon, as the day was dawning, the true light of the true day appeared. A young man cloaked in golden splendour appeared, holding out the banners of the divine flag, and thus he addressed Alfege. "Where are your feet taking you? Where is the urge to flee leading you? Where is your guide's malice taking you? Is this the way that leads to the crown – running away from the grip of the struggle? Is it possible for a man to glory in the palm of victory when he has not reached the finishing post in the race?" When the Saint replied that he was not running away, but was obeying the command of a divine messenger, the angel said: "That was not a divine command, but a word of diabolical spite. He did not want to rescue you from prison, but only to seduce you away outside the prison. The dutiful conduct of your former life weighs heavily on him, and so does your constant trust in the Holy Spirit, which is your consolation in these great troubles. The Spirit's presence gives men constancy; constancy gives victory, and victory brings glory. For that reason, the devil would rather try all his tricks than go away confounded by you. Return, my friend, to the place appointed for your heavenly crown. Know that the Father will honour you tomorrow in heaven with the very greatest honour, so that you may be with his son for ever." So Alfege, recalled by the angel, returned to the place, and happily awaited the hour when he would receive from God the Crown.

27. Alfege returns to his prison cell where he has a vision

When he drew close by, as he made to enter the grim cavern, he was seized by the rowdy gang of executioners and beaten with terrible blows. His head was struck repeatedly, and he was shut in his cell, semi-conscious. A fire was lit in the hearth to produce a stinking smoke. Once produced, it was fed and more material put on every hour of the day – for they thought to torture him with such punishments.

But God's champion remembered all that the Son of God had suffered for him, and thought that what he could endure for Him was of little account. The greater part of the following night had passed. As the Sabbath of the Octave dawned, an everlasting Sabbath was being prepared for Alfege in heaven. The dwelling of terror began to take on a share of heavenly grace, to exude perfumes of everlasting life, to echo with hymns tuned by the sweet voices of the Saints. That blessed man perceived these signs with great joy in his heart. He observed also Dunstan, one time Archbishop, glorious in his visage and his vesture. He was standing there and speaking with hands outstretched towards him: "Unconquered soldier of our Eternal King, we have come to honour you with our respect. We have been sent by him who has laid up victory for you from hatred, and has prepared an everlasting crown for you in heaven. Ah, whose company shall you enjoy after the death of the flesh? The citizens of the heavenly Jerusalem and the servants of God – if you endure patiently in your flesh your sufferings, which fall far short of Christ's. For we have seen the manifold troubles of the city: the burning of the temple, the slaughter of her sons, the dishonour done to you in your shackles, the tortures heaped upon you – twice as many as the kindnesses you have done. Accept whatever remains gladly, fortified by God's power! Know that the suffering of this time is no match for the glory to come, which will be revealed in you. For there will be this one day only for the punishment, but an eternal, everlasting day for the prize."

Meanwhile the knots of his chains were loosened, and the gaping of his gashes drawn together. Every wound to his body was made whole, and Alfege went his way dancing with the dancers and singing with the singers.

28. Alfege is taken from prison to the court

The watchmen were panic-stricken by the immensity of these wonders. They informed the men keeping guard on the fringes of the army that the place once damned with tremendous horror was now greatly blessed with visions of the gods. These men came running at speed, fell to their knees, leaning on the walls in their desire to see the present power of God. Swifter than speech they recoiled, struck by that very power. As soon as the leaders of the army had heard that their allies were flocking in droves from them and vying with each other to flock to the man of God, immediately they pronounced sentence of death upon him. They feared that if he lived any longer, their men would march in arms against them and they would perish more grievously at the hands of their own men than slain by men of other nations. Then a considerable band of armed men was sent and Alfege was led from the place of terror to the council of Wrath; from the dwelling of foulness to the judgement seat of Vanity. They knew that his feet had been virtually eaten away, from being shackled day in day out, so they placed him on a cart. They showed him this much humanity to hasten on the enormity of his sentence. So they dragged him to the synagogue of Satan. A huge wailing arose from the faithful who followed the divine knight with grief and groaning. In their midst he became a sight for angels and for men. He begged them not to stand in his way while he battled against the ruler of the world, but rather to give him the assistance of their prayers. Now there might come to your mind the son of God, either sitting on the lowly ass, or carrying the cross on his shoulders, the pitiful tears of the wailing women, the Pharisees tormenting him and the soldiers nailing him to the cross. When he was but an arrow's shot away, all the Council with a deep rumbling roared out these words: "Bishop, give us gold or today you will be a spectacle for all the world." Alfege, clasped respectfully by the hands of his friends, at first was silent for a little while from exhaustion. Then, once he had got his breath back he replied as follows: "I set before you the gold of divine wisdom. Abandon the vanity which you love, and turn your thoughts to the one true living and everlasting god. If you stubbornly scorn God's advice, passed on to you through me, you will die a death worse than Sodom, nor will you take root forever in this land."

29. The Danes attack Alfege; he is fatally injured

Then indeed the Devil's henchmen, with cruelty frothing on their breath, were no longer able to endure the weight of his words. They leaped forth from their seats with the spring of the swiftest lions, and struck the man with their axe-hafts. Then others severally flung stones at him. And now he was on the very brink of life. Thinking of Christ hanging on the cross for the good of all, he knelt down on his right knee and pressed his left foot on the ground, uttering this prayer both for himself and for those who tirelessly tired him: "Only Son of the highest father, Lord Jesus, who came into this world through the Virgin's womb to save sinners, receive me in peace, and pity these men." Then he fell to the ground, and rising again finally he spoke these last words. "Good Shepherd, only Shepherd: watch over the sons of the Church. As I die, I entrust them to your care." There came running up a certain man whom he had taken from the sacred spring. When he saw Alfege struggling still longer on the edge of death, moved by piety to an impious deed, he stuck his axe in his head. At once Alfege came to rest in everlasting peace, and directed his victorious spirit in triumph to the heavens.

In all the time since the Apostles, the first leaders of all the Lord's flock, what man lived more innocently than this one, or who ended his life more gently? Whose merits were ever so alike as those of this our champion and Stephen the first martyr? For both refused to plunder Church funds, both were most forceful in curtailing evil deeds. They were comparable in the manner of their death, equal in the love of their friends. Behold, these stones of the Sanctuary, once trampled by the feet of passers-by, are now joined with Christ, the highest cornerstone. He unites them from their different sources, making them one in him, in love, in desire, in beauty and in eternity!

30. The miracle of the oar blade

The leaders of the Danes desired to conceal both their wickedness and Alfege's glory. They unanimously decided that the Martyr's body should be sunk in the river, for they thought that the more his memory was taken away from men, the more the grossness of their crime could be concealed. But what the Dane contrived for his humiliation, Christ turned to Alfege's glory. For immediately a crowd of all the people, who under his teaching had cast off the error of their ways, took up arms and marched. They preferred to fall at the side of the dead man than allow the body, through which he had attained the mystery of holiness, to be handed over to be sucked into the river's eddies. So it was that that magnificent vessel, in which the Holy Spirit worked in many ways while he lived, was saved by one and all the people, and was neither drowned nor buried. Yet as the sun was just about to set, the Councillors of each side met, to decide by their debate an outcome to the great dispute. All agreed with the decision of the Council. This was that they should all beg the Saint, if he had any power, to show them the strength of his power at this critical moment. To put an end to the enquiry, the Danish enemy should choose the nature of that trial of strength. "Here is an oar", they said, "cut from an ash bough, entirely stripped of sap and bark. If the dawn should find this growing after it has been dipped in his blood, we too will agree that we have killed a just and holy man, and he will be yours to bury with honour. But if the wood remains in its former dry state, we shall say that out of your love for him you have made a mistake, and it will be up to us what we wish to decide about his corpse." All were content with the agreement's terms; the terms were followed by putting it to the test. So it was, in order that everyone should agree that Alfege was still living after death, against all the laws of nature the dry wood in the space of one night began to sprout. The stick which the Danes fixed in the earth in the evening, on rising in the morning they saw in full bloom. The Danes had no further power to contradict them. They rushed to embrace the dead man, planted numerous kisses on him, hung their heads and filled everywhere with their tears and wailing. The heavenly jewel was raised up on the shoulders of the rejoicing enemy. It was carried to the tree that marked his triumph, with countless wonders and signs revealed by the powerful strength of heaven. In a word, very soon health was restored to the infirm, bright light shed on the blind, the gift of hearing granted to the deaf; the dumb man received the organ of speech, the lame man walked with an even step. There a house of prayer was constructed over him, and many Princes of the Danes were baptised, reborn of water and the Spirit, and entered the heart of mother Church. When the rumour of his cruel death had winged its way to London, the strength of the signs also unloosed the tongues of all in proclamation of the martyr. Relying on their faith, they approached the Danes who were now made gentler towards the new religion. With a great deal of money and various settlements they contrived to become the keepers of his most holy body. The Danes had hardly agreed to their insistent demands, when they took their treasure – more valuable than all their gold – to London. No fewer than twelve thousand Danes and English accompanied him to the gate of the city, shedding bitter tears at the crime they had committed. From there he was taken up in a wonderful, dancing procession of the whole state, and carried to the Church of St Paul, Teacher of the Gentiles. Here he was acclaimed, honoured and laid to rest. In this Cathedral many years passed adding to the renown of his power. When times of peace returned, with his body intact he was raised by the great King Cnut, and translated to the Church of his Archbishopric – the church he had always loved in his lifetime, and which he had strengthened by his power; indeed, the Church for which and through which he had met his death. But any of the Danes who refused to be converted to the true, catholic faith even after the marvellous miracle of the green bough, was immediately seized by a ghastly scourge and died a bitter death. I could mention men lacerated by Demonic vexation, struck by ulcerous tumours, swallowed up by the sea, killed by their own hand. And something you would be even more amazed at: if anyone had taken any shreds of his clothing, he would reluctantly give them back after being terrified by an apparition in a vision at night – and after giving them back, he would die. O faithful evidence of truth! Evidence given to prove his worth! By his relics the faithful sick were miraculously healed; the faithless healthy were dreadfully scourged. All this I could tell, if I did not fear to wear out my readers.

But now, commending these words to almighty God, who alone can perform miracles, we must direct the course of our narrative to a closing speech. Great Alfege, soldier of a great King: you washed your robe in the blood of almighty God. Receive the prayers of your sons who cry to you. By your loving intercession, raise up those whom you have honoured by your holy suffering. Strong with divine assistance, you overcame the Prince of death: Father Alfege, make us strong against him, and help us to vanquish him. You had pity on those who stoned you: have pity on those who pray to you. Let your servants not know the gates of death and hell, but bring them to the gates of Paradise by the power given you by the Saviour, who lives and reigns together with the eternal Father and co-eternal Spirit, the one, only, true God; for ever and ever. Amen.

NOTES

1. Wisdom I.11
2. He was consecrated in the year 984, on the 18th September and enrthoned on the feast day of Saint Simon and Saint Jude, according to the Saxon Chronicle
3. Lower Italy
4. Bishop Kenwulf
5. King Ethelred had not yet reached his 46th year, if Florence is correct in saying that his father Edgar married his mother Alfryth in 964
6. Psalm 89 v.31- 33
7. see John 18 v.10
8. Maundy Thursday

Osbern's account of the translation of St Alfege from London to Canterbury

We have already recorded the worthy sufferings of the blessed martyr Alfege in a literary memoir. Those who were pleased to thank us for this have the most ardent longing and desire to know how his most holy body was translated from London to Canterbury. That he was translated there we touched on briefly in our account of his passion; but of the method of his Translation we gave only the slightest account. So let us recount it now.

In the 1012th year from the incarnation of our lord Jesus Christ, as the Saturday of Holy Week was drawing towards the evening, and the Lord's Day, the eighth day of Easter was dawning, the 19th April, the glory of the city of Canterbury, Archbishop Alfege, fell. His most glorious passion was for the good of all and at the same time shared with all who had been entrusted to him by God. He took on the unfading crown of everlasting glory, in the seventh year of his archbishopric, and the fifty-ninth year of his life. His noble body was taken up by the faithful (either out of grace or for a price), brought from the place of his martyrdom to the city of London, and was buried in the church of the Blessed Apostle Paul with countless glittering signs of grace. Soon health was restored to invalids, the blind were filled with clarity of vision, the gift of hearing was delivered to the deaf; the lame walked with steady tread, and divine blessings came very promptly to all who sought them. But as for the surviving authors of his death, the avenging wrath of God did not allow them to pass on without terrible judgement.

To cut a long story short, I set before you the following examples. Lord Haco fell on his own sword. A prophet intent on the science of astrology stuck a pen in his own throat. The Presbyter who insolently tried to steal the martyr's crucifix from his neck was slain by the hands of that same martyr. Another man of that same order, who rashly carried off his sandals, was assailed by a Demon and was dreadfully afflicted wherever the sandals dragged his feet, in the presence of all the people of the city of London. As a result of these events, so powerful a fear struck all the Danish Chiefs that the land could scarcely contain them. They abandoned themselves to the sea winds, thinking that they could escape the Martyr's wrath on the ocean, since the earth could not protect them from that wrath. Soon their oars foamed on the deep and they departed. A hundred and sixty ships were driven by adverse winds into deep waters and were sunk. But forty, and then a further twenty-five, were driven to unknown foreign shores, and were pitifully cut off by the same winds as if they had come there into a deliberate ambush. Yet there remained in England the wickedly bold Prince of wickedness, Thyrkill. His destiny was to plunder for a short time, but to remain in eternal damnation of the soul for his plundering. For when a little time had passed, there came Cnut, Chief of the Danes, with a fleet to England. Anxious that Thyrkill had managed affairs evilly and faithlessly, Cnut wiped out all that remained of his unspeakable people, just like wax tablets wiped clean with the stilus. As for the leader himself, the king banished him to Denmark with only six ships for protection. When he had landed there, the Chiefs of the Danes suspected he planned to raise internal wars. Thyrkill was immediately driven out from all the places of that region. Eventually he was killed by the rabble, and his body miserably thrown out to the wild beasts and birds. Thus were driven from land and sea those who killed the Archbishop, the Saint and honoured man known as Alfege.

However Cnut, the Chief of the Danes, saw that his people were being dreadfully and unremittingly slaughtered by the army of the English, and were now practically compelled to surrender on account of the difficulty of their circumstances. He summoned all those who had deserted to his side, and consulted them as to why so many adverse circumstances had touched them. They all replied unanimously: "There is a prophecy which the venerable Martyr Alfege made. When he was in the grip of cruel interrogation by your fathers, he predicted to them that they would not take root forever on English soil but would die by a death worse than Sodom. If you want to make him look favourably now on your times, bind yourself with this pledge. Promise that when there is a happy outcome of events, you will raise the venerable remains of his body from that place in which they are buried, and seek to transfer them to the Archbishop's seat, in the traditional ancient manner." So the Danish Chief assented to the advice of the senators, and following on the advice came a declaration of divine propitiation. For not many days afterwards Cnut obtained peace, then half the kingdom, and then the whole. When respite from all the tumult of war was granted, he remembered what he had once promised the Blessed Alfege. Straightaway he summoned Archbishop Egelnoth who at that time held the priesthood in the holy church of Durham. He was widely considered to be a holy and good man, particularly to the king because he had anointed him king with the holy oil. On the Saturday of the eve of Pentecost the Archbishop arrived in London, and sent word to the King, who happened to be getting into the bath at the time, that he was present and waiting to consider what the King wanted in the church of the Blessed Apostle Paul. On receiving the message, without delay he got out of the bathtub, covered his naked body in just a cloak, put simple sandals on his feet, and made his way like this to the Bishop with eager step. At the same time he gave orders to all the soldiers of his household, which they call Huscarls in the Danish language. Some were to start riots at the furthest gates of the city, others to take weapons and occupy the bridge and riverbanks, so that the people of London could not prevent their going out with the body of the Saint.

On entering the church the King embraced the Archbishop and kissed him. As soon as the doors were bolted, he said in a voice full of joy, full of fear: "Behold the day, which the Lord has made! On this day the treasury of the remains of Lord Alfege is to be transferred from the house of his rest to the house of his Archbishopric." At these words the Priest was more terrified than one can say, for he did not know for what reason the king had summoned him, and he spoke in great anxiety of mind.

"Almighty God forgive you, my Lord King, that you wanted to do this and yet gave me no indication of what you intended! I could have arrived better informed and prepared for everything. I should not then be in danger of dying, cut down in the midst of this great city! If you wanted to embark on such a difficult enterprise, why did you not at least bring men who could be assistants in such a task? The stone placed at the opening of the tomb is so heavy that it could scarcely be moved by many pairs of oxen, let alone be rolled away by the two monks who are the only others here. That is a foolish idea. Another time and other resources must be considered." The King had great trust in God and replied: "Holy Father, in this situation it will be very apparent that the Blessed Alfege wants to come along with us, if by his virtue he makes possible what is impossible for men. It has always been the way for extreme difficulty to give birth to a miracle. Let your holiness prostrate itself in prayer before God; let the monks go in faith to the mouth of the tomb. I shall lie in front of the doors as a gatekeeper." So it was that the priest's blessing was sought and given. One of the monks was Godric, who was once a pupil of the martyr and for some years afterwards a Deacon of the church at Canterbury. It is from him that we have received all these details, after careful questioning. The other was Alfward, who was nicknamed 'the Long-serving', as he had been a follower of the great Dunstan. On receiving the blessing, these two grabbed an iron candlestick, which was standing a little way off, attempting to smash the fabric of the wall of the upper structure which had been very firmly cemented. As those men have asserted, who have made God the witness of their assertion: the monks had scarcely moved their hands even slightly, when the smaller stones, cement and all the superstructure fell like leaves from a tree shaken by the first gale of winter. When they came to the stone that covered the opening of the tomb, they knelt down to the ground, put their shoulders underneath the stone and pressed against it, and soon they shifted it to another place with a slight movement. This is indeed more remarkable than credible, since as we said above, many pairs of oxen could not drag the stone, yet only two monks overturned it with just a gentle push. The King and Archbishop came running up, awe-struck with admiration. Tears ran from their eyes as they gazed inside and saw that Alfege, that instrument of the Holy Spirit, lay incorrupt and that there was no trace of decay in his entire body. Calculating the number of years, they found that it was the tenth year from which the Saint had been buried. The King cried out aloud for joy, and poured out his prayers together with his tears. "Most Holy Father, sweetest of all delights; most Blessed Father, precious beyond all the world's treasures: have pity on this poor sinner! Do not hold my initial unworthiness against me, nor the cruelty that my ancestors inflicted on you, a just and good man. I admit you are the most powerful ally of the eternal King, and as long as I live I shall count you as my advocate. Save me! Save us all, as you were saved by eternal salvation! Bring your sons great joy, and set out on the journey with us!"

However as the Highest Priest of God came nearer to clasp and raise the venerable body in his arms, his mind was in turmoil as he could not find a board anywhere on which it could be placed and brought to the ship. While he was standing hesitating in great desperation, he noticed a wooden board laid under the body exactly the right length and width to fit the body's measurements. It was just as if the original builders had placed it there for this sole purpose, namely that the Saint could be lifted from there at some time without any difficulty and with no damage to his body. Happy and joyful beyond all expectation, they took the winding sheet, which Godric the Archbishop's chaplain had brought with him for the burial, and they wrapped his holy limbs in it, together with the wooden board lying underneath. But since part of the body still remained uncovered, one of the monks ran to the altar of Saint Paul the Apostle, and seizing the altar cloth which lay on top, placed half a pound of gold there in payment for the cloth. Running quickly he went back to wrap whatever remained. Then the precious treasure, the precious body was lifted up on the shoulders of the monks. They went down in single file along the road which led to the river Thames, with the King and the Archbishop following them, each of them with his entire mind turned to God. Now as they began to approach the river, the royal ship sailed up to meet the Martyr as he came. It had golden dragons on the prow and was filled with soldiers. The King leaped into it more quickly than you could say, and took the Martyr in his outstretched arms; then holding out his right arm he helped the Archbishop in. Soon when the ship had moved a little way out from the shore, the King sat down holding the tiller, steering the ship to the opposite river bank. Then you would have seen that the great power of God looked with favour on the Martyr's ceremony. You would have seen the bridge and riverbanks all strewn with armour clad soldiers here, while there at the furthest gates of the city you would have heard the shouts of the feigned riots in progress. You would have seen the King steering the ship, the noble crew pulling on the oars, the Archbishop praying and the holy monks displaying their devotion. As soon as they came into shore, the King was the first out of the boat. He took the body and placed it on a carriage. He sent this on ahead with a sturdy band of soldiers. He himself was sitting on the furthest edge of the bridge with the Archbishop, until those who had gone ahead were further away from the city. This was because he feared attacks from the citizens.

Then getting up and teasing the Archbishop with playful remarks, he said: "Thanks to me you have been freed from danger of death – something from which you thought you could not be freed. Now make your way, safe and sound to the Saint, and humbly pray him to show us his favour in these times of ours. I should go with you, if I were not busy with – as you well know – great affairs of state. The Queen is in residence in Kent with my son Hardecnut. I shall send word to her to meet you with all the nobles."

After parting from the King, the Archbishop followed those who had gone ahead, taking with him a huge crowd of Huscarls. When he had got so near that the men ahead (who were constantly turning to look back behind them) could see a cloud of dust raised up the sky, those very men at the front suspected that citizens had come out of the City. Hurriedly they sent on ahead the attendant monks and the martyr with a small escort. They themselves however came to the village of Plumstead, and took up their position in a confined area. They offered three prizes for the three squadrons, their minds made up to die for love of the Blessed Martyr. But once they were close enough to see the Cross on the standard, they recognised as companions those they had feared were enemies, and found greater joy than they had imagined. So they pressed on and stayed that night in an estate, which is called Earthea. As they did so, a vast crowd from Kent came to meet them. There were infantry mixed with cavalry, women with men, young with old, individuals leading dances through the throngs and playing on harps, as if escorting the ark of the Lord's covenant in triumph. You may be certain the sons of Israel sang no differently when the Prophet Moses led them through the middle of the Red Sea with dry feet, or when King David brought the ark of the Lord from the midst of Aminadab into his city.

When the citizens of Canterbury heard that Alfege, their Father in life and their companion in death, had arrived, they were just like Jacob, woken from his deep sleep when he heard about Joseph. They burst into floods of tears for joy. They leaped up to meet him, rejoicing because they were able once again to see the man whose blessings their parents had experienced abundantly in his life as much as in his death. Above all people, the monks of Christ Church rejoiced while they adorned the Temple for the solemn festival and put on their ritual priestly vestments. Some brought bells which jingled as they scurried about; others held lanterns, Gospels, gem-studded crucifixes in their hands; and with their voices raised in chanting they went in procession to meet him. Then he was carried aloft with a wonderful dancing procession of the entire population of Canterbury. He was translated to the church: not that of St Paul, Teacher of the Gentiles, as once he was, but to the church of the Saviour of all. This was the church which he had always loved during his lifetime, had strengthened by his courage, on whose behalf and with whom he had sustained death. He was carried in not as if newly acclaimed but in honour as if living with God for all eternity. Thus he was placed there.

When the third day dawned, Queen Emma arrived with all the nobles who were with her.

Numerous gifts were offered of various precious kinds. She blessed the living God who had brought Alfege back to honour and glory of his name with such great magnificence, whom the enemy had blasphemously taken away with such great shame. So that the most holy Father might show some spark of his grace to his sons, seven days later he returned the power of speech to a dumb man. Also, a little later he freed another man who was bound in iron chains by breaking the iron.

These are the joys of today's festal day; that is the day's ceremony. For these reasons it is decreed that every year it is celebrated in the church of the Saviour at Canterbury in the Diocese of Canterbury on 8th June so that it may not be forgotten through any oversight how the Blessed Martyr Alfege was deemed worthy to be brought to his own land from elsewhere. And although we celebrate the day of his passion in common with all in the community, we above all ought to celebrate the day of his translation. For on the day of his Passion we had one simple cause for rejoicing, but on that of his translation we received the gift of a two-fold joy. On that day we celebrate his being raised up into heaven; on this day we celebrate both his being crowned in heaven and closer to us on earth. Blessed be the Son of God, who crowned him in heaven and gave him to be close to us on earth, who with the Father and the Holy Spirit lives and reigns, God forever and ever. Amen.

NOTES

1. "In the year 1014. Cnut was elected King by the Danish settlers in England in place of Swan who had recently died. In 1016 after the death of Ethelred the King the majority of the English chose him King. In 1017, when King Edmund left the land of the living, he held sole rule. Yet his fellow Dane Thyrkill had not yet gone into exile. In 1021 he was banished by Cnut to Denmark, together with his wife Edgitha, just before the Feast of St Martin. This is according to the Wigorn, Dunelm and Westminster manuscripts." (Wharton)
2. "Osbern has miscalculated. That year was the eleventh since his death. All historians are agreed that Alfege's body was translated in the year 1023." (Wharton)
3. i.e. Erith
4. "From this it appears that the account was written in the Christ Church Canterbury in accordance with custom on the anniversary of the Translation of Alfege. I also think that that his Life was written by Osbern on the day of his Passion. For Eadmer writes (Life of Anselm, book 1) that Archbishop Lanfranc authorised an Account of Alfege given by Osbern, and laid down that the authorised work be read and sung in the Church of God." (Wharton)

Bibliography

The Anglo-Saxon Chronicles
Nicholas Brooks, *The Early History of the Church of Canterbury:* Leicester, 1984
Christ Church from 597 to 1066
M T Gibson, *Lanfranc of Bec,*Oxford, 1978
Gibson, Heslop and Pfaff, *The Eadwine Psalter,* Pennsylvania
William Noel, *The Harley Psalter,* CUP, 1996
N Ramsey (ed.), *St Dunstan: his life, times and cult,* Boydell, 1992
David Rollason, *The concept of sanctity in the early lives of St Dunstan* (in N Ramsey op.cit.)
R W Southern, *Eadmer: Life of Anselm,* Clarendon, 1972
W Stubbs, *Memorials of St Dunstan,* London, 1874
E. Temple, *Anglo-Saxon Manuscripts 900-1066*
Alan Thacker, Deerhurst lecture, given in September 1994
Alan Thacker, Cults at Canterbury (in Ramsey op.cit.)
H. Wharton, *Anglia Sacra,*1691
Woolley (ed.), *The Canterbury Benedictional,* 1955

Chronology

953/4	birth of Alfege
?	entered Deerhurst Priory
?	monk and prior at Glastonbury
?	became Abbot of a community at Bath
984	succeeded Aethelwold as Bishop of Winchester
1006	succeeded Aelfric as Archbishop of Canterbury
1007	travelled to Rome to receive the *pallium* (a robe, the traditional symbol of his authority) from the Pope
1009	held Council of Enham at which disciplinary rules were passed
1011	The Danes overran Kent; attacked Canterbury in the autumn and took Alfege prisoner
1012	killed by the Danes at Greenwich on Easter Day (April 19th); his body taken to St Paul's, London
1016	Cnut became King of all England
1023	At Cnut's instigation, Alfege's body was translated to Canterbury, arriving on June 8th and placed on the north side of the altar in Christ Church a week later.